CW00394822

Emerging Leadership

The challenges you will face and how to overcome them.

Dax Murphy

Contents

Introduction

What exactly is leadership?

This is a big question, especially as you progress through those emerging leadership roles. Anyone in first management appointments up to middle managers are emerging leaders and how these years of your career are navigated will create the blueprint of how successful a leader you will become.

If you are an emerging leader, this book is for you.

This book shares the collective expertise of 300 leaders across the globe, who are currently working at director level positions in their respective companies. Some have shared their own leadership stories and others have selected the common mistakes they have witnessed in up and coming leaders. All have offered their advice on how to overcome these common obstacles. All of this feedback, knowledge and advice have been collated into easy to understand sections with the common themes that came from these leaders.

This book doesn't promise to reveal the "Golden Rules of Leadership" that is common place in business literature.

Instead, this book promises to share real leadership advice, from real leaders in real situations - as you will see there are many different elements that emerging leaders will face. The intention is for you, the reader, to learn and gain inspiration from the sections that matter to you, in your leadership role.

There is no need to attempt to replicate everything in this book, it is not a list of rules - it is advice from people who have been in your position and want to help.

So what is leadership?

It is different things to different people and at its best leadership can change cultures, industries and lives! Emerging leaders can become illustrious leaders - those that make a valuable, tangible and important contribution to their followers and to the world around them.

Good luck on your leadership journey...

The Challenge

Emerging leaders become development and relationship snobs.

They focus all of their energy on those in more senior roles and lose sight of the lessons they can learn from those around them, thus creating huge gaps in their leadership capability.

The Solution

Can those in junior roles really coach those in senior roles?
Is it true that the more senior role you hold, the more capable you are at developing others?

Thinking about it now, you will have likely answered "Yes" to the first question and "No" to the second. We answer like this because intellectually it appears obvious - anyone can be a coach and it doesn't mean you are good at development, just because you have a high profile job.

Yet this approach is often neglected by emerging leaders - in fact the opposite is true. An emerging leader is often reluctant to actively learn from their juniors or peer group. Preferring instead to target those in senior roles to gain feedback and coaching.

Let's be clear - seeking personal development and coaching from those in more senior roles can be tremendously helpful and transformative. So it is important to utilse this resource. However, personal development from your juniors and peers can be equally helpful and transformative and to ignore this will slow your growth as a leader. Also support from juniors and peers is often easier to access, so those that leverage this can rapidly accelerate their own leadership journey.

If emerging leaders can learn from all around them, why do they limit themselves to those in more senior positions?

A good example of this, from one of the leaders I interviewed, was:

"I worked for a manger that wasn't particularly great with people. He set clear expectations of what was to be done, the exact steps to be taken and measured those steps meticulously. He didn't set a vision, trust or challenge appropriately, yet he was keen to progress his career in leadership.

It was obvious my manager was frustrated with the engagement levels of his team, so I offered my support and advice. This offer was refused, rejected and I was told "how could I help with something I couldn't understand?"

Two years later, I was promoted into a Talent Development role, where coaching conversations were a part of the job. Then the craziest thing happened, the manager who had refused my support a year ago, came to me and actively wanted help with the challenges he faced. Of course I worked hard to facilitate his development and over time he developed into a great leader (and he eventually got that promotion he always wanted).

Here is the problem - If that manager had utilised the capability within his own team (me), he could have developed his career at least two years sooner than he did."

It is a powerful lesson to learn - so from now onwards; will you actively learn and seek development from all around you or just from those with the right job title?

If you can commit to learning from all around you, then you will invariably receive some valuable learning, become a better leader, manager or person quicker than you could ever do by relying on those in senior roles.

The Challenge

Emerging leaders fail to create an autonomous environment for their teams.

Many emerging leaders make the fatal mistake of thinking leadership is about the leader and therefore try to ensure everything is done 'their way'.

The reason why this is fatal is because leadership is not about the leader - it is always about the followers.

There is no such thing as a leader without followers. What many emerging leaders fail to realise is that followers are not automatically the people who work in your team. They work because it's their job - they will only follow when they decide to.

The Solution

Create an autonomous environment for your team. An autonomous environment creates intrinsic motivation. This is the type of motivation where desirable behaviours last forever, not just while they are measured or rewarded. The behaviours stand the test of time because when you are intrinsically motivated, you fully believe those behaviours to be critical, true and linked directly to your personal values.

Intrinsic motivation significantly increases the effort and attainment of teams. This is easily proven, as you personally know this to be true.

Take a moment to consider the amount of energy, passion and focus you give whilst engaging in activities you love.
Now think about how much energy, passion and focus do you put into the things you are ordered to do.

You probably found the answer to the first statement easy to answer - you give as much as you can to the activities you love.

The answer to the latter statement may have been more complex. You will either comply with a sufficient amount of energy to deliver on the expectation and only do the task whilst it is being measured or you would rebel and demonstrate counter-productive behaviours. Neither answer would be positive for the follower, leader, customer or company - this is why leaders need to generate intrinsic motivation.

Imagine a world where your team puts in maximum effort and delivers maximum attainment, just because they believe it's the right thing to do. **Because they believe in you.**

Is this a realistic goal?

The answer is an emphatic YES, by creating an autonomous environment that builds intrinsic motivation.

The word autonomy scares many business leaders; they think this will lead to chaos and failure because there are no rules or regulations. This is not the case and is simply a misunderstanding of the word. Autonomy is mistaken for independence, where employees would work with no set goals, targets or guidelines. That would create chaos in a team environment!

In an autonomous environment followers still have rules, still have to work together and still have to aim for a clear and specific vision. The autonomy comes because followers decide, within set remits, on how they will deliver on the vision and goals.

Autonomy is the ability to choose HOW to achieve the vision.
If you can communicate a compelling vision to all of your team and if you are prepared to ensure your followers understand the goals and the remit they can work in, then you can create an autonomous environment. Your followers will then become intrinsically motivated and become a truly high performing team.

The problem is most emerging leaders are pessimistic about this concept because they believe people will just take advantage of your trust. So they never commit to developing an autonomous environment. They don't allow autonomy, which in turn reduces engagement, reduces potential and reduces performance levels.

To a certain extent this pessimistic view is true - some people will take advantage, HOWEVER these people are a massive minority and will be extremely easy to identify, within an intrinsically motivated and engaged team. There is nowhere to hide in an autonomous environment, so as a leader you can support these individuals in the appropriate manner.

Don't make the mistake so many emerging leaders fall into. Instead make trust and autonomy the most vital aspect of your leadership. If you do, it will provide intrinsic motivation, followers who believe what you believe, more engagement, more effort, more attainment, more creativity and more opportunity for you to emerge as a magnificent leader.

The Challenge

Emerging leaders mistake coaching for directing and therefore never enable their people or teams to reach their full potential.

The Solution

Firstly, recognise coaching is a highly skilled and complex process. Most leaders have never been correctly trained, yet most believe they are experts.

Many leaders mistake **management** (clearly defined expectations, provide rewards and consequences, then deliver a result), for **coaching** (facilitate how a person thinks about an area that creates a self-motivated behaviour change).

This creates a wonderful opportunity for emerging leaders.

If you invest in your coaching skills and improve your effectiveness, you will set yourself ahead of the crowd.

The first solution - invest in professional coaching qualifications to improve your skill-set.

Secondly, below are four behaviour strategies that will instantly improve your coaching effectiveness.

1.

It is VITAL to have great goals, over a timeframe. For best results, only agree one great goal and have a timeframe that is longer than one or two monthly meetings.

The key thing to understand is coaching takes longer than just telling someone to change, **however**, coaching delivers results that stick long-term and that will out-perform any directional leadership.
A good activity to help create the great goal would be to ask, who you are coaching, the following:

"Imagine what great would look like if you were watching it on video, now describe it."

2.

IT IS NOT ABOUT YOU! As a leader it is absolutely understandable that you will be invested in the person you are coaching. It is plausible you could have feelings or thoughts about their success being your success.

This mindset has the potential to tempt you into the world of persuading, cajoling and influencing.

That is not coaching. At best it's feedback. At worst it is bullying!

However, it is about the follower. They might miss the target, they might not "get it".

They might smash the target, they might "get it" better than anyone believed possible.

Either way it is not your fault or your potency. Coaching is the art of allowing people to see from their own point of view the changes to be made and the actions to be taken. As a leader, the very best you can do is allow this to happen, what happens after is not about you.

3.

Approach the person and situation like you know they have already be made aware of the changes needed in the past and probably tried to do something about it.

If you do this, then the focus automatically changes to how you can help the individual get a different result this time. You know they have been given advice and feedback before, so there is no point in repeating that process. The approach now becomes that of a journey together, of walking alongside the person you are coaching.

4.

Pay attention

BIG, MASSIVE, INTENSE, ATTENTION!

The bottom line is as a coach or leader we have to understand the person's perspective, we need to understand how they receive and react to each moment. If you give all of your focus to the individual you are coaching, the level of information, commitment and improvement in yourself and the individual being coached will go beyond expectations.

The Challenge

Many emerging leaders fail to keep their dreams and vision alive during the tough times.

Up and coming superstars look and act fantastic when things are going their way, but when the going gets tough, when they get rejected or when circumstances go against them, they lose belief and confidence quickly.

They stop looking and acting like superstars.

The Solution

Here is a fundamental fact: EVERYONE who has achieved success in their lives, has had tough times, has been rejected, has lost and has been told they are not good enough. The simple truth is to become a successful leader you have to overcome these obstacles.

The difference between becoming a successful leader or not will ultimately rest on how you psychologically define the challenges that inevitably will cross your path.

Hard times will come. You will struggle. Sometimes you will fail. How you define your struggle and the tough times will ultimately determine if you give up or if you push through.

Embrace this truth - success is not easy. It is not owed to you. It is not given out. Success can be achieved by you once you decide nothing will stop you, no matter what barriers present themselves.

Here are three ideas that can help you get through the tough times:

1. **Visualise** - see, feel, hear, touch, taste, understand and live though the moments you want to achieve.

Don't just visualise the successful moments though. It is powerful to visualise the winning post, the fanfare and all those amazing feelings once you achieve your goals.

HOWEVER, don't forget to visualise the tough times and even more importantly how you will grow, focus and drive through the challenges you face. Visualisation is about preparation - prepare for the whole journey rather than just the end goal.

For example: A marathon runner visualising the finish line is important and positive. It is also equally important to visualise the 13 mile mark and how you pull on your inner strength to push through the pain barrier. The runner who visualises the whole journey is better prepared for the whole marathon.

Spend some time visualising your goals and vision. Visualise the whole journey, the struggles, the knock-backs, the pain and visualise how you will overcome them, how you will make your decisions and then visualise every detail of how amazing your life will be when you finally achieve it.

2. **Research leadership**

In this day and age, the majority of managers tend to be lazy concerning their self development. They either assume they are good enough, that they will learn on the job or that their business will give them the training they need. If you want to become a great leader, you have to take accountability for your own growth and learn how to become successful.

There are people who have achieved what you want - there are literally blueprints to create your best leadership style. You don't have to reinvent the wheel, research those who have achieved what you want and role model their behaviours/strategies.

The more you fill your mind with the strategies of those leaders you deem successful, the more you will understand how to create your own successful leadership style. You can effectively stand on the shoulders of giants and propel yourself to the next level in your leadership.

3. **Build a feedback network around you and utilise them**.

It is a good idea to test your ideas and get feedback before you take away the safety net. Having a network that provides feedback before you take action in the real world, is beneficial.

Getting feedback on the actions you will take can make you more productive, more self-aware and more focused on the actions that will make the most difference. The key factor is that you must control who this feedback network is, choose the people you trust to be honest, the people who have your progress as their focus rather than any other agenda.

The Challenge

In our ultra competitive world, every opportunity to impress counts, especially with those you meet in positions of power within your business.

The pressure is on... how will you be perceived? Will you be funny? Intelligent? Insightful? Confident? Boring? Stupid? Shy?

What do they want to hear? What will they be interested in?

What type of person do they connect with? Do they want to talk business? Small talk?

AHHHHHHHHHhhhhhhhh!

How on earth can anyone make a good first impression when they have all that going through their mind?

They can't... and this is the failings of many emerging leaders.

The Solution

When emerging leaders put significant levels of energy into second guessing what senior leaders want to hear, it dilutes authenticity.

Think about yourself, when you are at your absolute best and most authentic. Were you thinking of all the things you should and shouldn't be doing or were you just acting naturally in the moment?

Of course you weren't second guessing everything or having a mind cluttered with a list of worries, actions and assumptions. So, why deliberately clutter your mind when meeting senior leaders?

Here are 3 approaches you can take that will help make that great impression and be able to influence senior leaders more effectively.

1. Don't try too hard!

Trying too hard will have the opposite effect you desire. All the energy and focus you will burn up while trying to second guess every comment, every movement will literally drain you of all creativity, playfulness and energy.

That will equal a worse, fatigued and unenthusiastic version of you. That was probably not the look you were going for.

Good questions to ask yourself before interacting with someone new could be:

"If I KNEW that the relaxed, authentic and playful version of me can connect with anybody in the world, how would I act right now?"

or

"If I KNEW the person I am about to meet thinks I am totally amazing already, how would I act?"

2. Utilise your physiology to create certainty

Being confident in these situations is important. You can create the feelings and emotions of absolute certainty and confidence at any given moment.

The key is in your physiology. The way you move, the way you hold yourself and even the way you breathe. You can literally train yourself to feel good or feel bad.

How to test this theory:

Remember your worst work day ever. The day that everything went wrong and you seemed to upset or annoy everyone, you were rubbish at your job and your boss had literally just told you so. Remember the details.

Now think about how you felt that day. Feel how you held your shoulders, see how you walked through a room, and think about your breathing… was it fast? Slow? Deep? Shallow?

Now think of the opposite. Think about the day you were absolutely unstoppable. The day you got the promotion, aced that presentation, smashed that target. The day everything you touched figuratively turned into gold!

Feel how you felt. Step into that feeling. How do you move? How do you walk? Talk? Breathe? That strong, fast, intelligent, capable you. See how you looked, feel what you felt, think how you thought.

Did you see the difference? Feel the difference? Your physiology drives your emotional state.

The differences might have only been small, but there were differences. Recognise these.

If you want to be confident, then consciously step into the unstoppable you. Hold your body like you did, breathe like you did, walk, talk and laugh like you did.

You will feel more confident almost immediately!

3. Be curious

A simple approach. Be interested in the person you are meeting. Show a genuine curiosity in who they are, what they do, how they feel. There is nothing more appealing than someone who gives you their full attention that is fully focused on you, who isn't distracted from anything but you.

When you meet people, just be interested in them. Give them your attention. Be curious to find out more. You will make the most positive impact you could ever make.

The Challenge

Not being able to change a person's behaviour, when, said person, has demonstrated undesirable behaviour previously and has been accepted.

It is a challenge that will face all emerging leaders at some point in their growth journey. This can surface for numerous reasons, be it previous management neglecting to confront the person or a change in company approach etc.

How do emerging leaders ensure that this issue is handled appropriately and also gets the desired result? Giving this type of feedback can result in an emotive, emotionally charged and counter-productive reaction if handled incorrectly. And this is where many emerging leaders fail.

The Solution

If you go in with a sledge-hammer you could end up with a fight on your hands and potentially lose this individual as a follower - remember, just because some behaviours need to change, does not mean they are not highly capable and skilled individuals.

However, if you go in with a soft approach the individual could miss the message entirely or not believe that it is important to adapt.

Here are four common approaches that have proven to be extremely successful.

1. Courage to act

Common sense, however sometimes common sense isn't common practice. The biggest single regret from emerging leaders is that they wish they had acted sooner. The longer you procrastinate, the more the behaviour is deemed acceptable and the bigger the issue will seem when you finally do take action.

Once you have witnessed the behaviour, make the decision to challenge and discuss quickly. This doesn't mean reacting in the moment without being prepared, (not being prepared is a major mistake!) it means you make the decision to have the conversation quickly, prepare appropriately and have the conversation in the shortest timeframe possible.

2. Acknowledge the issue has not been challenged before.

As a leader it is important you take accountability for any past failings, even if they had nothing to do with you. Taking accountability and acknowledging this hasn't been appropriately dealt with, will remove any emotive feelings and blame from the individual concerned. Allowing them to effectively "let go" of any past failings and look towards alternatives in the future.

Your ability to take accountability for something that was not your fault, might pull on your ego. Don't let it. Don't play the blame game, it doesn't help any aspect of the situation, in fact it just makes the situation worse.

The blame game is like drinking poison and hoping your enemy will die. As a leader, you must envision the future rather than dwell the past.

3. The past is the past

It is also vital to ensure the individual who needs to change their behaviour clearly understands that there is nothing that can be done about the past, so there is no need to try.

Whatever the behaviour was doesn't make them a bad employee or an evil person. If you leave the individual feeling like there is no way back, then they probably won't try. Make now and the future the focus. The world of opportunity is open, the future is exciting and all that matters is what happens now.

Allowing the person to feel and know that there are no grudges and that the past is forgotten, will give them time, space and enthusiasm to make the difference.

4. The future thinking approach

Always look to build motivation and excitement within your feedback. Allow them to envision how amazing the world will be, how the team will work better, how the results will accelerate, how great your relationship will be.

With a future focused approach, together you can generate a sense of WHY it is important to change, HOW that change will look and be achieved and WHAT the benefits will be for all concerned.

The Challenge

Emerging leaders are focused more on avoiding failure rather than seeking success.

It is an ultra competitive world. Businesses demand ever improving results and performance measures are expanded.

The meaning emerging leaders give to these expectations will change their actions, decisions and feelings dramatically.

So what are you? A failure avoider or a success seeker and why does it matter to your health and well-being?

The Solution

A success seeker will focus on being the best they can be. They are not jealous of others' performance, rather they are keen to understand how to improve. They are also happy to share their strategies and techniques to help others' performance.

A success seeker wants to do good and be good.
On the flip-side, the failure avoider is focused on other people's performance, with the goal of not being the worst.

They show jealously when others are successful and you will hear them making up excuses for why others have done well "it was just lucky" or "it's easy to improve when your results were bad before" are the types of sentences you will hear them say.

There is no chance they will ever share what has worked for them, because that gives them the upper-hand. Unless, of course, it has the opportunity to make someone else look bad, then they will gladly share as it proves they are better.

How to identify what you are:

<u>Success Seeker</u>
Positive attitude
Creative and sharing
Focused on own performance
Wants to improve
Will take risks to progress

<u>Failure avoider</u>
Negative attitude
Copy others and hide best practice
Focused on others' performance
Wants to be better than someone else
Will never step out of the boundaries

Which are you?

I have been both in my lifetime. This has depended on my situation, confidence and environment. It doesn't mean you are a bad person if you are a failure avoider and it doesn't mean you are totally awesome if you seek success. It is just the meaning you give.

If you try to avoid failure then your focus is on others' performance, so you can ensure you are not the worst. You can't control others' performance, so if others have a good day, you feel awful and if others are struggling you feel good.

That's a massive problem.

If you focus on the things you can't control it will only bring stress, anxiety and panic into your life. I am sure you know the physiological and physical health problems that come with stress, anxiety and panic. In simple terms they are killers.

When you seek success it's different.

Being focused on improvement, on making progress is the recipe for happiness and fulfilment. You feel better, you relieve yourself from worry, so that you have lots of energy and enthusiasm to DO good! Not only that, because you are trying to improve you will improve, so will ultimately get better results!

Choose to be a success seeker. It's more fun, less stressful and you give yourself much more chance of being happy, fulfilled and successful.

The Challenge

Emerging leaders fail to identify the critical factors that will determine their personal success and fulfilment. Therefore they are more susceptible to burn-out, depression and anxiety, which ultimately leads to a limited leadership career.

The Solution

Some leaders appear to have mastered and created a life filled with joy, satisfaction and fulfilment. While others live with a life of pain or dissatisfaction and struggle.

The myth is that only a few leaders are lucky enough to be truly successful and the majority are destined to miss the mark. This is not true, we all have equal opportunity given to us. So what stops most leaders? What stops you?

The truth of the matter is you let the distractions in your life determine your success - This is where most fail. Here are the most common types of distractions that we allow to take us away from what is important to our lives and leadership.

The Urgent

The factors in our life that demand our attention. For example, the external demands of the jobs we do – tasks, objectives and goals which are other peoples' agendas, all of which appear to need our attention right now.

Then there are other distractions such as other people asking for your time or to take on work for them.

We perceive that these things need our attention NOW... they masquerade as important, they grad our attention and our focus. It is a never ending, forever growing, a mountain of tasks, jobs, roles and things to do!
Then we flip from one extreme to the other. We spend all of our days rushing around delivering on these urgent tasks, then when the day's work of other peoples' agendas are done, we are so exhausted we need to "unplug" and get away from our busy lives, so will "veg-out" in front of the TV with a glass of wine.. or three.

The Unimportant

With 'the urgent' taking up so much of our lives, no wonder we "veg out" with the TV/games console/social media or we eat poorly or get away from it all by drinking or smoking. We do this to escape.

Here is the problem with escapism... and it's a big one.

You are literally wasting your life, burning your success and emptying the glass of fulfilment... AND you can never escape for long anyway, so it is futile.

Do you know those big goals you have? They are really important. When you spend all of your time being distracted by urgent things and unimportant things, you will NEVER become the successful leader you desire.

I have personally spent a good deal of my life in this distracted state and I absolutely understand how easy it is to find ourselves in that place in our lives. It isn't a good place. It is limiting you. There is another way:

The Important

Magnificently, successful leaders have one significant difference from the un-successful.

FOCUS. They focus on their important goals with laser sharp proficiency and because they are focused on the important, they take the appropriate action, which in turn ultimately leads to achieving those goals. As an added bonus because they are focused on the important rather than the urgent, they don't have to "unplug or "veg out" as making progress on their important factors GIVES energy rather than draining it.

Crystal clear focus on the important = more opportunities = more action = more achievement = more energy!

It is a simple formula, but can it work like that in reality? Is it plausible to just stop doing our jobs, tasks and roles just because they are distractions for our important goals? In reality we have bills to pay and those urgent distractions help pay those bills.

Agreed... We have a reality and that will involve urgent factors and tasks. However, the trick is not to become absorbed and distracted by these unimportant elements. Yes, they have to be done, but honestly could you spend more time on the important things in your life? More time progressing towards your true success and fulfilment?

If you don't create this time... you will fail. In leadership and life.

Consider the following as an example:

Can you ever feel fulfilled and completely successful if you drop the quality time with your loved ones so you can focus on work and get promoted?

Some unfortunate people think that when you get that more senior job with the bigger pay packet, they will THEN be able to make it up to their loved ones. They believe that when they get promoted THEN they will be fulfilled. Please don't be one of these people. It is a ridiculous belief system, which is clearly unfounded. Success is a feeling... not a job... not a destination... not an amount of money... It is a feeling that you can create.

And the fact of the matter is, you CAN have both the quality time with loved ones and get that promotion. In fact, you will have more chance of the promotion and of being successful in your role if you create the time for the important things in your life. It nourishes you. It feeds you. It makes you better, stronger and more agile.

The only way you will become the leader you desire is if you demand and dedicate time to the most important factors in your life. Loved ones, personal growth, whatever it is... it is important for a reason.

Please don't let your life disappear in the urgent and wasteful zones. Instead live an exceptional life. Focus on the important things. Don't wait until tomorrow... Do it now.

Start small if you need to, just take action everyday and you will see amazing things happen to the quality of your life and your leadership.

The Challenge

Emerging leaders focus on forging a career and forget about being an unforgettable boss to those that follow them.

The solution

Keep focused on being the best leader to your followers that you can possibly be!

It is simple advice, but the best, if you truly want to become a great leader.

To become unforgettable will depend on each follower. Today, I want to share my experience with the best boss I have ever had. The reasons why I will never forget him and always aspire to be as good as him. Hopefully this can supply some inspiration:

Passionate

His energy and enthusiasm for his work, for me, for my people and for life, was unbelievable. There was a natural vibrancy and energy in him that wasn't fake. He had this power to lift my mood, my energy and desire to new levels, just with his passion - The extra work and effort he got from me, just because he was enthusiastic was amazing.

He had my back

He made me and the rest of his team feel safe. I have seen so many leaders in the past look for a fall-guy and someone to blame if things went wrong. This was never the case with him. He would ensure we all knew he would protect us if needed and would publicly defend his team with ferocity.

What this allowed was for his team to be brave, innovate and creative. He gave us the freedom to take a few risks, because we knew he would never throw us under the preverbal bus. He enabled his team to become the most innovative and successful team in the whole company. We changed how that company did business for the better.

Played the long game

He always pushed me to think about the decisions I was making on the longer term. He often used to ask how the actions I took today would affect my business in five years time.

Most leaders think very short term, because of the way most businesses are set up, leaders would normally never think past the current financial year, more commonly the current quarter. The ability to think differently and long-term allowed me to make significantly better decisions and take value-added action.

In making me think longer-term he automatically gave me time and space to do the right thing for my company and my team.

A boss that has the courage to allow their team to think long-term is very rare and totally unforgettable.

Authentic

Authenticity is a term that is thrown about in many leadership philosophies and is obviously very important. How I saw this in this particular leader, and have never seen this since, is that he acted and spoke to me in the same way as he did to his boss or the board.

A boss who has the confidence to be themselves in any situation and also treat his employees that same way he would treat the company VIPs was so powerful.

Didn't sweat the small stuff

He always put things into perspective and never panicked, even when everyone else did.

I vividly remember failing to correctly budget payroll for a month, at a time when the whole company had made this the number one focus. I was embarrassed, angry and I informed him how upsetting this was.

His response was to say, "Has anybody died? Well there is no need to be so upset then."

It brought me right back to earth, calmed me down and taught me that making small things seem big only causes stress and worry. Which is never the right way to overcome a challenge.

I hope you can see why this leader made such an impact in my life. He was an unforgettable leader... and I hope you become one too!

The Challenge

As I developed through my leadership journey, I had big decisions to make in my career, leadership style and life. To cut a long story short, in those early years I messed up and made a lot of mistakes.

As my experience and leadership career has grown, I have often seen other aspiring leaders make bad decisions that slow down their progression. I have often wondered how much my emerging leadership journey would have differed, if there were guidelines to help me make better decisions.

In an effort to ensure you make better choices than I did, here is the advice I would give to myself early in my career.

The solution

1. Make Decisions!

Surprisingly, one of the biggest problems I faced was how to be decisive. I was so afraid of getting it wrong, that I wanted the perfect answer. I needed to understand every possible perspective and unearth every single fact before committing to a course of action. This is a futile pursuit. You will never know all the facts and you can never be certain of a result.

My advice - make the decision and make it quickly. The faster you decide, the more opportunity of getting the right result you have.

Don't let issues build and build. They turn into mountains very quickly, so dealing with them early will work out so much easier in the long run. This doesn't mean to ignore or forget about gathering information, of course you have to have an idea what you are dealing with.

Just don't procrastinate on taking action, be bold, be brave…

ANY ACTION IS BETTER THAN NO ACTION!

2. Be able to let go

It is absolutely vital that once you have made a decision and taken a course of action, that you review if it is working on a regular basis. If it is not working, change what you are doing.

Be able to adapt your decision.

Too many leaders will be decisive and make a decision, but then they will stick to that course of action no matter what. Even if the outcome is not desirable. The concept that you have to be perfect in your decision making needs to be let go. It's not true, however what can be true is that you learn from the actions you take and adapt them accordingly to ALWAYS get the desired outcome.

Don't be focused on being right. Be focused on getting it right.

3. Ask great questions

The questions we ask ourselves will determine the answers we get in return. Ask better questions and you will get better answers. Most leaders will have an internal dialog that becomes self-fulfilling. For example, if the internal voice is based around fear, the decisions you make will probably be influenced accordingly. The trick is to get that internal voice focused on solutions -

The questions I ask myself, when making a big decision are:

> *What decision will make me feel the best?*
> *What decision will be the best for the people around me?*
> *What decision will be the best for the wider world?*
> *What decision will I be proud of?*

When making your next big decision, write down these four questions and then spend some time answering them. It will lead to more success.

4. Copy other peoples' success!

Whatever decision you have to make, there is someone in the world who has been in your situation and become tremendously successful.

We are more connected in this day and age than we have ever been before. Locate the experts, find out what they do and replicate it, with your unique spin on it. The hardest way to solve any problem or make any decision is to start from scratch, without any support or advice.

Starting from scratch is deliberately putting yourself at a disadvantage for no good reason. Find out what the best in the world do, then role-model that! Those leaders, who are the best in the world, aren't magic, they aren't super-human, they have a process. Learn the process, apply the process and you will get similar results from that process!

The Challenge

Emerging leaders prefer to remain big fish in small ponds. They tend to measure themselves against their peer group rather than seniors. They enjoy being the influencing member and highest performer of the groups they associate with.

This limits their overall performance levels to those they surround themselves with. If you are serious about becoming a world-class leader, then surround yourself with people who are already world-class."

The Solution

At this very moment, you are leading to the level of those you are in proximity too. You will take on the habits, attitudes and behaviours of those around you.

This means, as an emerging leader, you have to be extremely careful who you choose to spend your time with.
When you do choose, align yourself with the leaders who are already masters in your business, you will learn from them, grow with them and automatically raise your performance levels.

Align yourself with people who think like you. Who have a purpose like you. Who lead like you want to.

Most emerging leaders don't live up to their potential because they fail to lead the way they aspired to. Most emerging leaders complain and moan about how hard it is to make a difference and become influential. All the while compromising their talent to 'fit in' to their peer group.

The fact that you are reading this book, will probably mean you are already a high-performer or at least aspire to be. You want more, you know there must be more. You have passion, purpose and vision.
Now you have to unleash that potential. This will take drive, persistence, hard-work and resilience. This is why it is vital to align with people who believe the same as you. People who are currently performing, better than you. We all need help, we all need support, surround yourself with the very best leaders you can and you will accelerate your personal growth.

Take a look at the five leaders you spend the most time with. You are the average of these five. If you want to become world-class, then the very first hurdle you have to overcome is who you spend your time with.

Who are those people in your business, or world, that are significantly better leaders than you? These are the people you need to spend your time with. Learn from them, grow with them... Don't be afraid to be the lowest performer in your group... It means you are going to improve your game dramatically!

That is how emerging leaders become world-class. By learning from those who already are.

The Challenge

Politics in business are difficult to navigate. The balance between managing cross-functional relationships and progressing your own objectives is difficult to master. The problem I see many emerging leaders face is how they build relationships with people who are challenging to influence or that they just don't like.

Not being able to manage relationships across the business, especially with those notoriously difficult individuals we all face in our lives, can be particularly damaging to an emerging leaders career.

When emerging leaders find particular people, especially challenging and rude, the commonly deployed tactics are to either fight fire with fire, defending their cause to the death and reflect the rude behaviour OR they retract inwardly, making sure their interactions are at the minimum they have to be.

Neither is a good strategy.

The Solution

1. Understand what a "difficult person" is.

A difficult person in your life is a person who has a different perception or perspective than you and will communicate that in a way that pokes at your value system.

For example, if a key value you hold is respectfulness and you believe that the way to demonstrate respect is listening to the other person without interruption - then you find that someone who continually interrupts you with disagreements to your perspective, you are likely to find that person difficult to deal with.

So with that in mind, it is important to appreciate the fact that other people can have a different perspective than you **AND YOU CAN BOTH BE RIGHT.**

2. Ask "What is going on in their world at the moment?"

The overwhelming majority of people will see themselves as 'the good guys' and do not deliberately spend their lives trying to be a difficult, obnoxious person! The reality is that there will normally be an external stress or pressure somewhere in that person's life to cause the bad behaviour. Except this and you can easily stop taking their actions as a personal attack.

One personal example of this has stuck with me. I once opened a door to get into a building and a woman walking the other way barged past me without a word. I was offended by this rude behaviour instantly shouted "Thank you" sarcastically at her. I later found out, from a friend, that she had just been told that her son had been in a serious car accident and was rushing to the hospital to find out if he was okay.

Who was the difficult and obnoxious person? To my dismay, it was me.

Don't take bad behaviour as a personal attack - see it as a person who is having difficulties and struggles instead.

3. Ask "What does this person need?"

As described above, bad behaviour is rarely something people deliberately enforce on others. So understanding that the difficult person you are dealing with, needs help or support is important. Do they need a break from the discussion? Do they need to be listened to? Or maybe they need encouragement?

4. Listen to understand… Don't listen to defend!

Listening to defend is letting the other person speak, just so you can gather more information to argue your point!

This is literally useless and will not improve the relationship one bit!

Understanding others point of view is critical in building relationships, gaining trust and creating a collaborative working relationship. It is common sense, unfortunately common sense is rarely not common practice. The key factor for you is to take accountability. It is your job to listen to them, it is your job to understand them. Do not expect them to listen to you first, that is not your job or theirs.

5. Clearly communicate your own perspective.

We assume everyone knows what we know and see what we see. This is a common mistake.

Don't assume they see ANYTHING the same as you - people are not mind readers, don't expect them to be.

I remember a time two leaders had an argument about the colour they should have the boardroom office painted (Yes -really). They were both in the room, analysing the test colours on the wall and based on where they stood in the room the colours looked slightly different from each person's perspective. The argument stopped as soon as they both stood together, thus seeing the room for each other's perspective.

They assumed both could see the same as the other... Never assume!

The Challenge

Emerging leaders neglect the importance of small talk, thus limiting the level of connection and influence with those around them.

The Solution

As human beings there are various levels of engagement we will commonly use to build relationships. In its simplest form, communicate and work on five levels, which are all equally important:

1. **Re-charge** - Relaxing and reflecting, this is normally conducted when on your own and is about mentally refreshing.

2. **Chit-chat** - Basic social interactions about trivial matters.

3. **Deeper 1-1 conversations** - Being fully present, emotionally and intellectually engaged with someone who shares similar values.

4. **Multi-task**- Focusing on a number of tasks at a given time (you probably spend a lot of time in this zone while working!)

5. **Flow** - One subject, with deep focus and attention. Many emerging leaders have a significant problem with one of these levels. Small talk.

Whatever you want to call it, chit-chat, gossip, tittle-tattel - it is those conversations that are conducted socially and are usually about superficial matters.

Many emerging leaders find this level of conversation the most difficult to apply in a work related context. It is easy to understand why many people hold small talk in low esteem, as on the surface these types of interactions add little value and therefore most emerging leaders try to skip the small talk in order to get onto deeper, more meaningful topics.

This is a critical error. The emerging leaders who try to skip this level have failed to realise that chit-chat is fundamental for building relationships and trust. The concept of discussing in depth subjects without having made a small connection with previously, is a big turn-off for most people.

For most emerging leaders, this means that they rarely get to have the deep and meaningful conversations that they desire because they tried to jump right in at that level. Without first connecting on a more superficial level, this will usually lead to disappointment.

Skipping the small talk will create an impression that you are either very intense or just plain weird.

The fact is, small talk is easy.

You won't go wrong if you just pay genuine attention, listen carefully and ask clarifying questions. We can all do it. It is just that some leaders undervalue it because it appears to lack depth.

But it doesn't lack depth, the analogy that resonates with me is to see small talk like trying on a relationship - just like you would try on clothes in a store. Small talk is a risk free environment where you can assess each other in a non-threatening or judging way, to see if you have rapport and get along.

If you do, then the deeper more meaningful conversations will follow. If you don't, both parties can remain at a superficial level with no harm done to anyone's feelings.
If you want the big talk, the meaningful talk, pay attention to the small talk, it is the doorway to deep and authentic connection.

The Challenge

Imagine if you had the tactics to connect successfully with all of those around you. To win their hearts and minds.

It is not as easy as it would seem. I recently worked in collaboration with a CEO of a well-know company, he was struggling with motivating and engaging his team. This gentleman was an extremely talented and intelligent person, with an academic history that most people only dream of. Yet his wider team, although they understood clearly his goals, were lethargic and disengaged.

Looking from an outward perspective, the problem was obvious. He was a logical, evidence-driven communicator. This was the style of communication he naturally preferred and therefore that is how he communicated. In affect he won the minds of his people... but not their hearts.

I am personally the opposite in the way I communicate; my natural preference is to communicate to the heart, with passion and enthusiasm.

However to be an effective leader, you will need the skills to communicate in a compelling manner to the heads and hearts of your followers. You need the ability to adapt our style dependant on our audience and the subject matter.

The ability to consciously identify what style to use in each situation, will be invaluable in improving your leadership.

The Solution

When and how to win hearts:

This is about connecting with people emotionally and is particularly effective when:

- Building interest on a new idea or concept
- Gaining support for a decision that has already been made (i.e. launching an initiative that has been signed off by the board)
- Raising passions and performance on a current way of working
- Leading a team that is struggling and low on moral

There are many ways to win the hearts of your followers - Ensure your communication includes vivid descriptions, so people can visualise. Also use metaphors and stories, as these are extremely powerful and easy to empathise with.

Therefore creating a connection and understanding in a visceral manner.

When and how to win minds:

This is about connecting with people in a logical, well-articulated manner, with thoughtful positioning and analysis.

The best times to utilise this communication style are:

- When trying to persuade anyone of anything! At some point in the discussion a logical argument will be required.
- Persuading a change in direction on something already decided
- Advocating one decision over another
- Addressing highly complex or technical sets of problems

In the process of winning the minds of your followers it is imperative that your message has been carefully constructed.

Things to consider are; describing the situation, why the subject needs attention, common ground for all parties, proof and benefits.

Emerging leaders need to be aware of and capable of both strategies as most leadership situations require both the hearts and minds of followers.

The Challenge

Many emerging leaders think because they are the leader, they have to make all the decisions, they are always right and have a team culture that complies.

They create cultures where everyone follows... blindly, compliantly and obediently.

The Solution

There is not one leader in the world who is brighter, smarter or more aware, than a team of people working together for a common purpose. The fundamental truth is, a team of people who are 1. All working towards the same goal and 2. Are able to challenge for the common good, are statistically more likely to make better decisions, than one person on their own.

A culture of following a leader blindly can creep up on you. Yet you should avoid it at all costs. It will erode at your team's performance, sometimes forever.

A story I was told by one of the leaders I interviewed emphasised this very point:

"About fifteen years ago, I secured a leadership role in an exciting brand, but the team that I inherited had worked in a culture of following the leader without question or input.

They didn't think for themselves and they expected to be told what to do, all of the time.

This created a massive problem for me. I was new to the company and I didn't have the knowledge to be able to tell them what to do. Therefore I had two options:

A. *Learn everything in the business really quickly, then create brilliant ideas on how to perform better and then tell my team what to do ... step by step.*

B. *Assume that my team, on the whole, had the capability and knowledge to perform, (as they had performed well over the previous two years) then trust and empower them.*

I decided to go for option B.

Firstly, I replaced 'To-do' lists with a vision. I explained to my team what we would look like in the future, what we would achieve in the future. I made it bright, I made it bold and I made it something that I personally believed in.

I then asked my team "How should we go about achieving this vision?". Rather than telling my team what to do, step by step, I instead gave an intention on our destination.

For example, our team vision became to deliver world-class customer service. My team then told me how we would achieve this.

My team changed from a group of people who waited to be told what to do, to a team of people who decided what to do for the best interests of the vision. The ownership of decision making switched to them.

There is a clear rule about when a leader can give ownership fully - The team has to be capable to deliver the task in hand and understand the vision. If these factors are not in place the leader's job is to first either train capability or communicate the vision in an understandable and compelling manner.

Once my team took on this ownership, they started thinking for themselves, they became more engaged, they felt more valued and they became more productive.

Then the obvious happened:

My team was a group of two hundred capable people, who were focused, connected to each other and acting like decision makers.
All of the other teams in the company had one leader telling two hundred people what to do and when.

It doesn't matter how creative, intelligent and smart the other leaders were. My team was two hundred times more creative, motivated, pro-active and intelligent... My team became unstoppable!

My team then out-performed every other team on every measure within the company - We had the best customer experience scores ever, the highest engagement scores and grew year-on-year profit more than any other team in the company."

Leadership is not about commanding and controlling followers - Leadership is about giving control and creating leaders.

The Challenge

Emerging leaders think they are surrounded by expectations about how they should behave, what success is and what it isn't. Leadership is a tremendously serious activity, so emerging leaders tend to behave in a serious way.

Why do this? Who sets these expectations on our leaders?

Why is it all so serious?

What if the expectations we live to are wrong? What if they don't enable your leadership?

The Solution

Maybe being foolish is the path to success...

Only a fool would lack good sense and judgment

Wisdom is just a clever excuse for being cynical. The cynical never try anything new, because they already think they know everything and new things are doomed to failure. They will use their wisdom to find the excuse to keep on doing the same thing they have always done.

Fools will try the original and don't know something can't be done.

That is how emerging leaders change the world, by doing what can't be done!

Only a fool would see the world with wonder and curious eyes

Fools will see opportunities in everything. They are grateful for the world around them and see everything as positive. Imagine if you could see the positive in everything in your life.
Imagine you could see the opportunities in everything. The possibilities that become available to you will become endless.

Only a fool would make loads of mistakes and risk failure

As sensible people we all know that failing is not success. We think it is appropriate and sensible to do what it takes to avoid failure at any cost. The bottom line is, this will make us play safe.

The foolish, on the other hand, will risk failure. They will reach high and they will learn from their mistakes along the way.

To achieve anything of significance, you will have to risk failure and sometimes you will have to accept failure. As long as you keep on learning and taking action, you can achieve the truly significant.

Only a fool would work hard even when the objective isn't clear

We are told it is important to have crystal clear goals. SMART objectives are everywhere. Why on earth would anyone work hard when we don't know the outcome?

Fools just work hard at everything they do. They know that total control is just an illusion and because of this they discover opportunities that would be unavailable to those with ridged plans.

Only a fool would seek out fear

Nobody likes fear, it's not fun and it is scary.

The fool realises that facing fear, being comfortable with fear is the number one catalyst for personal growth. Be foolish and reach your potential or play it safe and become mediocre.

Only a fool would not worry about the past or the future

We spend so much time worrying about the past and planning for the future, we forget about the only real thing we have - this very moment!

Yes, it is important to learn lessons from the past and have dreams for the future, but we shouldn't spend all of our time in either time zone!

The fool enjoys the present, the amazing world we have right now. The present, right now, is reality. It is precious and you only have right now to enjoy it. Grasp it, use it and be grateful for it.

The world will tell you to grow-up, be serious and follow the script... don't fall for that.

Learn as much as you can and don't be afraid to be foolish!!

The Challenge

Emerging leaders often fail to leverage elite productivity, substituting being busy instead.

The Solution

Focus solely on a singular objective until it is completed or you reach a specific milestone. Then move onto another task.

To put it another way - multi-tasking simply does not work - don't even bother trying, it will make you less proficient and less productive. It is a scientific fact.

To prove it do the following test: Get a stopwatch and time how long it takes to complete the following two tasks:

1. Multitasking test - Count out loud to 100 while writing down the alphabet twice, at the same time.

2. Singular focus test - Count out loud to 100 while writing down the alphabet twice, but this time count to 100 first, then completing the writing task afterwards.

Your result will demonstrate the same as anyone who has ever tried this - the singular focus test is faster.

Focus on just one thing at a time and you will move quicker and perform better. Here are some ideas on how to apply this to your leadership:

Scrap to-do lists

There have been many studies on this and the results tell us that 41% of the average to-do list doesn't get done.

High performing leaders utilise calendars and time blocks instead. They attribute a full days worth of objectives into time blocks. This enables you to stay focused on one objective at a time. Because you have blocked out time for each objective, it frees up your mind to focus on the task in hand, rather than jumping from one objective to the next.

Never ever sacrifice quality time

This is so important. To be ultra productive you need to be at your very best. This means the quality time in your life is vital because it will re-charge your batteries, boost your energy levels and freshen your perspective.

When returning to your tasks after quality time, you will be more energised, quicker-thinking and at you most productive.

Unfortunately most leaders will sacrifice quality time because they don't think they have enough time to deliver on their objectives. So the strategy is: More work and less play.

The problem with this strategy is obvious - the more you deny yourself the quality time you need, the less productive, less energetic and less creative you will be!
Give yourself quality time... You will deliver more, deliver it quicker and at higher quality.

Only deal with email/social media once per day

Here is a fascinating statistic: People who access their email or social media within the first 40 minutes from waking up, are over 25% less productive that those that don't.

Don't try to kid yourself that you have to regularly check emails, just in case of an emergency. The chances of that happening will be ridiculously rare. If it's an emergency, people don't normally contact you via email or social media!

Instead of intermittently distracting yourself throughout the day by checking your inbox or you phone, block out time on your calendar for emails and social media.

Have a positive morning routine

Almost every single highest performing person in the world, will have a morning routine that pro-actively and consciously sets them up for an ultra productive day.

You already have a morning routine. The question is, does yours set you up for a great day? If not, why not?

Morning routines of high performers vary. Some people meditate, others do exercise, many write positive affirmations for the day or a journal.

Each person's routines can be different, however the desire is the same: create a positive and conscious intention for the day ahead.
When you prepare to have a great day and set positive intentions, the more opportunities you will have of delivering a great day.

Maintain peak physiology

The more energy you have the more productive you are. Therefore the highest performers in the world focus on how they treat their bodies. Ensuring they eat healthy, drink lots of water, sleep at least 7 hours per night and take breaks to relax.

It is common sense advice, but it is often ignored. If you are tired, dehydrated, undernourished then you will not be in peak condition… **If** you want to be at peak productivity then you need to be in peak condition.

High performers know this and utilise this to their advantage.

The Challenge

Emerging leaders, at some point in their careers, will start to believe the 'hype' and let their ego balloon to unattractive proportions.

One of the leaders I interviewed was infected with a truly massive ego. She was totally in love with herself and her ego.

During the interview, she consistently informed me of how fantastic a leader and person she was. The stories ranged from her exceptional performance at school, to becoming a 'big player' in the business world. According to her, she had done it all... perfectly... every time.

The thing is, she is not the only leader I have met who had a big ego. If you are honest, you have probably met a few yourself. In fact, you can probably think of a leader in your business today that has a massive ego.

Or even worse... maybe, just maybe, someone reading this would think of you?

"Our ego hinders our ability to influence more than anything else under our control. Ego is the biggest reason leaders fail."

Michael McKinney

- When a leader's ego grows to the point where they believe they always have the right answer - **A leader**

will fail.

- When a leader's opinion matters more than their follower's opinions - **A leader will fail.**

- When a leader stops listening and stops learning - **a leader will fail.**

- When a leader surrounds themselves with people who continually confirm and conform to their will and pander to them - **A leader will fail.**

Ego is the mortal wound of leadership. It distracts you from the foundational truth of leadership. **The best leaders in the world, bring out the best in other people.**

<u>The Solution</u>

Ego isn't a real thing. It is just an idea. An idea of who we think we are and who we believe we are.

This idea tells us:

"Who I am is what I have."
"Who I am is what I have done."
"Who I am is what other people think of me."
"Who I am is how much stuff I own and how much that stuff is worth."

An ego, in the simplest of terms, believes that it is separate from everything else and in competition with everything else.

As leaders we need to be aware of our own ego and evolve it, so we become great leaders that serve our followers.

The three levels of ego evolution

Dr. Wayne Dyre, explained that there are three stages of ego evolution in adulthood and I think these have clear links to leadership.

The Athletic.

This is based on "What you look like, is what you are". It is simply a narcissistic view on life. **It is about looking good, rather than doing good.**
You will see this in leaders that will attempt to take the credit for other peoples' ideas and work, in order for them to be seen in a positive light. You will hear these types of leaders continually discredit other people too. This is to make others look bad, in order to elevate their own status.
It is clear that possessing this type of ego will detrimentally effect your leadership. **It will erode trust, loyalty, respect and authenticity**. All of which are critical to leadership.

The Warrior

This is the most common version of ego you will find in leaders. This is all about being the best. It is about competing, fighting and being the number one.

In moderation, this can be beneficial to leadership. But when it grows into a self-fulfilling, ever growing and unstoppable ego, then it becomes disastrous.

Believing you are always right and surrounding yourself with only people who say you are right, is frighteningly bad leadership.

Logically, how can any one person be smarter, better and more intelligent than a whole team of people? The simple answer is they can't. Yet with a warrior ego, a leader won't listen to others' opinions. They will lose engagement, value and commitment from their teams.

The Statesman

This evolves from 'What can I get' that you find in the latter two stages, to a **'How can I serve?'** focus.

At this stage a leader understands that they are connected to their teams and followers. **Their success is the growth and development of their people.**

As a servant, a leader will gain: trust, loyalty, respect, authenticity, engagement, value and commitment from their followers.

They will also instantly tap into the collective mind-power and ideas of the whole team, which the Statesman leader, understands is far greater than their own individual intelligence.

Why does leadership fail?

An Athletic or Warrior ego is the most common reason why leaders fail.

What level of ego evolution do you live and work at?

Are you in it to look good? Are you in it to be the number one, have lots of power and make all the decisions?

Or are you in it to serve those around you? To create the environment for people to flourish and grow?

The Challenge

Emerging leaders don't know when to quit, so will often lose valuable time and development chasing lost causes.

The Solution

This view is the complete opposite of the advice emerging leaders are given. Don't quit, keep fighting, push through are the mantras that are told.

So, is quitting ever the right thing to do?

I hate to say it, but sometimes the answer is 'yes'.

Many successful leaders will consistently preach that we shouldn't quit. That the formula to success is to keep on taking action towards your goals.

When you review the recipe for success, taking action everyday is the most common ingredient. If any of us are going to be successful, then the reality is we have to take action towards our goals.

So how does quitting fit in to the recipe of success?

What if you are trapped in a situation that is restricting your progress, limiting your potential or suffocating your dreams?

Is it right to stay and fight in that situation?

Well, if your current struggle is a part of the journey towards your personal goals, then YES you should stick it out and keep on taking action to keep on getting better.

Have an honest look at the bigger picture of your life, is your current reality just a bump in the road or is it a dead end?

Ask yourself:

'Have I changed and adapted myself to maximise this current situation?'
'Have I tried everything? What else could I try?'

If you haven't changed your approach and your mindset, then you shouldn't quit! If you want to change ANYTHING in your life, start with yourself first!

However, there are those times you should quit.

Ask yourself:

'Does my current reality have a fundamentally negative impact on my life goals?'
'Have I changed myself in that situation, to try and improve it?'

If you have a negative impact in your life, that you can't change by adapting your mindset... then quit... now.

Life is far too short to spend it being miserable. If you cannot chase your goals, if you cannot become the best version of you, if you are trapped and being restricted then you HAVE to do something about it.

Think about it, at the end of your life will you regret chasing your goals or would you regret not trying?

The honest truth is, if your situation is suffocating your potential, then you can quit and **you will** find a better environment.

If you go to work hating every second, without any hope of improvement... Quit... Find another job! The longer you stay, the less confidence and self worth you will have. That is no way to spend your working life! The same goes for relationships in your life... If there is a relationship that is hurting you, which is having a negative impact on how you live... then quit. You don't have to stay in a relationship that hurts!

You can quit and become happy, successful and fulfilled.
Don't live a trapped life. Live your life to the fullest.

Become the best version of you.

The Challenge

Many emerging leaders become the person who always wants to help and support everyone around them.

They keep on giving and giving to others. Even to the point they compromise their own agenda and well-being.

If this resonates with the type of leader you are, **I have good news:** You are a caring, kind and loving person. The desire to help others is perfectly normal and it is a fantastic attribute to demonstrate.

I also have bad news: If you ever get to the point where you are physically tired and mentally drained because you are sacrificing yourself, this is a negative way to live your life.

In fact you might even be digging yourself an early grave.

The Solution

What is needed is greater balance in your life.

Understand Your Needs.

Spend time to reflect on what you need personally to feel good and energised. Be clear and specific, write these elements down and ensure you make them a part of your life everyday.

Think of this list like the safety advice you get before take-off on a plane. They always tell you that if the air masks are released, to put yours on first before helping others, this is because you are in a better position to help others when you are not suffocating!

This principle works in leadership too... The best, most capable version of you is more able to help others effectively, than a run down, tired and stressed out version of you.

Work out where you really add value

Spending your time trying to do everything for everyone isn't productive or helpful. Spend some time to figure out where you can make the biggest difference and focus your attention on that. Imagine how much value your leadership will add to those around you if you spend your energy on things that truly make a significant difference.

> *"If it doesn't add value, It's waste."*
> Henry Ford

In leadership, you will discover that 20% of the actions you take will create 80% of the output you want.

Therefore, if you have a job list of 10 things to-do - Two of the items on this list, once completed, will deliver 80% of the productivity and performance you desire.

Say 'No!'

If someone asks you to help them and it doesn't allow you to reach your personal needs OR it doesn't fit into the important 20% of actions that will add massive value, then say 'no'.

You have permission to say 'no'.

Saying 'yes' to everything and everyone means you don't value yourself and you don't value what you can give to others. Say 'no' more often means you will add more value and it can also save you from burning out.

In conclusion

Serving those around you is an inspiring and wonderful way to live.

Just remember that to significantly help others, you have to be at your best. This means ensuring your wellbeing is a big priority.

Also, it is important to know where you can add the most value and then place your focus there. You can add real tangible value, if you focus on the important stuff! Don't waste time on being busy, that is a game you can't win.

Finally, learn to say 'no'… It will free your time, allow you to be at your best and allow you to help others at an advanced level.

The Challenge

Emerging leaders never reach their potential because in the tough times leadership itself will feel counterintuitive, having to give your power and control away to be truly successful - Most emerging leaders never grasp or connect to this concept.

The Solution

How many great leaders have you worked with in your career?

If you are lucky you might be able to count one or two.

How many people in leadership positions have you worked with or for, who are not great leaders?

This is, of course, a significantly larger number.

So why, if the desire for great leadership is in such high demand, is it not more abundant in the business world?

We could point to the way companies are set up – they need results very quickly so therefore only focus on the short term, whereas great leadership is a long-term proposition.

Another perception is that because it is so rare, we believe that great leadership is reserved for the uniquely gifted. Those special few, who have magically been born great leaders.

I suggest that neither is true... I suggest that leadership is rare because it is counterintuitive.

Counterintuitive is a proposition that does not seem likely to be true when assessed
using intuition, common sense, or gut feelings.

A useful example to explain a counterintuitive proposition, is to think about driving a car when your vehicle starts to skid. In this situation you will usually feel the rear end of the vehicle shifting unexpectedly to one side. You will then need to identify which way the rear is moving, and then steer into the skid. So if the rear is shifting towards the right, you should steer to the right. If the rear is shifting to the left, steer left.

This of course feels counterintuitive as the instinctive reaction is to steer away from the skid.

Leadership is the same...

No matter which leadership model resonates with you, the simple truth is that when you are a leader you will need to trust your followers and your followers will need to feel trusted.

We all know the ability for a leader to trust is critical. Yet in reality this will feel counterintuitive.

The concept of giving up control is frightening. The facts are, that as a leader you are accountable for the results achieved, so giving up control to your followers will appear very risky.

Apply this into the skidding metaphor. As a leader you have ensured your team are capable, trained well and understand your vision. When things are going well, you will be free to trust your followers to work autonomously. This is, in our metaphor, when you are driving your car in a controlled manner.

Then, the car goes into a skid - the pressures of delivering a plethora of results, behaviours or actions exhorts the leader into a sense of urgency.

The instinctive reaction for the leader is to try to take control of the situation. The sense of urgency will feel real and who better to know how to navigate this than the leader themselves? Therefore they will remove the autonomy from within their team and take a more direct and controlling approach. This is just like the instinctive reaction when in the skid, we will automatically want to steer away.

The right thing to do is continue to trust and to believe in your followers. But just like steering into the skid, this is counterintuitive. As long as you have ensured they are capable and that they understand the destination, then how your followers deliver has to be autonomous. After all, your followers have more collective knowledge and skill than you do. So if you really want the best results give your team the best working environment.

People, who work in an environment where they are trusted, trained and valued... will always work better and harder than those that aren't trusted.

You know this to be true; because that is the way you work best.

Yes it feels much more comfortable to take control, but that isn't to the benefit of your team. And a great leader knows their entire job is solely to be of benefit to their team.

The next time you feel the urge to control, remember the car skidding metaphor and you will know how to ensure your leadership doesn't fail.

The Challenge

As an emerging leader it is critical for you to grow a high performing team.

You will need a team that is cohesive, that works for each other and for the greater good. A team that is comfortable and secure enough to challenge each other. A team that welcomes new ideas and originality, rather than following the accepted standard.

Unfortunately, creating this type of team is easier said than done.

The Solution

Adam Grant, in his book 'Originals', has a chapter dedicated to the science behind which leadership strategies create the highest performing teams.

Adam Grant reveals five common strategies that leaders use to build their teams. Which one do you use?

Professional

The aim is to **recruit and attain the best skilled team possible**. Whatever the task in hand is, this type of leader will seek out the highest skilled team possible. This team will then be **given challenging tasks and autonomy to deliver on them**.

Star

The leaders who utilise the 'star' strategy, don't concern themselves with the specific skill set of their team members. What these leaders are interested in is **the future and potential of individuals within their team.**
They will **seek out the brightest, sharpest people, who demonstrate the brain capacity to become world-class** at what they do. Within this approach, the team will be given **challenging tasks and the autonomy** to decide how these tasks should be accomplished.

Commitment

This strategy is based on **cultural fit.**
The leader will build a team of people who share the same values and beliefs as themselves. In essence the leader surrounds themselves with people who believe what they believe. This team will be **lead with high challenge, autonomy and strong emotional bonds** to the mission.

Autocracy

This approach shares similar attributes as the professional strategy. The focus is on skills, with **individuals with the highest skill set being the most desired.** The difference in this approach is, rather than allowing their teams an autonomous environment, this strategy leans heavily on **financial based incentives and micro-management.**

Bureaucracy

This strategy is based on **recruiting and growing a team based on skills**. The difference is that these teams will be managed with challenging tasks combined with very **detailed rules and regulations** on how to deliver on these tasks.

What strategy should emerging leaders choose?

A high performing team is a team that will push each other, can challenge one another and which will welcome new ideas and originality.

Hopefully it is obvious that **Autocracy and Bureaucracy won't generate a high performing team**. These approaches would only deliver average results and create conforming and non-challenging team members, due to the micro-management and rules and regulations management style adopted.

If you have a basic level task, which you need a low level of performance and you don't want your team to think about what they are doing and how to improve on it, then Autocracy and Bureaucracy are the options for you.

However, if you want a high performing team, then you are left with three options... **Professional, Star and Commitment**.

The most commonly adopted approach is **Professional**. Get the highest skilled people possible. On the surface this is a reasonable assumption to make.

But it's the WRONG assumption to make - The research clearly demonstrates, this approach is the worst at building high performing teams out of the remaining options. The shocking truth is that it is at least **three times more likely to fail** than the others!

The second most popular approach is **Star**. Building a team of people, who have the capacity to grow and become world-class appears seductive.

However, the **data once again shows us that this is likely to fail** - twice as much as the last remaining option...

Commitment.

This is the least adopted strategy by leaders across the world, yet the data proves, time and time again, that this approach is the most likely to produce a high performing team!

Why does a Committed strategy produce a high performing teams?

- They demonstrate more **passion and intensity.**
- They believe in the same things as the leader, so everyone is **emotionally bought in to a shared vision.**
- Being surrounded by people who share the same values automatically create a strong sense of **belonging and loyalty**.
- A team that is emotionally connected and driven will be more **willing to speak up and share new ideas.**
- Those **ideas are more likely to be accepted and listened to**, because everyone knows that the best interests of the team are at heart.
- **Making the right decision** for the team, **takes precedence over any ego or status quo.**

No matter which strategy was your preference when we started - we all know that a team who share values, beliefs and feel trusted will perform.

Skills can be taught, beliefs on the other hand can not... Surround yourself with people who believe what you believe and you will have a high performing team.

As Adam Grant says in his book **"Skills and Stars are fleeting, commitment lasts".**

The Challenge

Your team doesn't respect you

The solution

"Everything would be okay if it wasn't for her."
"She is fine to my face, but then stabs me in the back."
"She thinks she is better than me."

This is what I was told repeatedly while facilitating a high performance coaching session with an emerging leader. All she wanted to talk about was how one of her assistant managers didn't respect her, as she said, "She doesn't have my back, I can't trust her."

Respect is important to us all. As a leader. As a manager. As a human being. **Respect is vital.**

We all want it, the question is, are you willing to do what it takes to get it?

Respect is not given to you. Even when you are in a senior role at work, that doesn't mean you automatically receive respect. People might work for you, but they don't have to respect you.

Respect has to be earned. If you want more respect in your life and are prepared to put in the hard work, then here are six reasons why there could be a lack of respect in your life and what to do about it.

1. You Don't Respect Yourself

The leader I coached lacked self belief. The way she talked about her situation and her job, was like she didn't quite feel like she deserved it. She didn't think she was good enough or capable.

In simple terms, she didn't respect herself as a manager and her Assistant Manager knew it. Speaking to her, all she really needed was to understand that she had been given the job because her boss believed she was good enough. That simple realisation was all she needed.

If you lack respect for yourself, here is my advice: To purposefully review all the good you have done, you are an amazing person who has been through a lot. That deserves respect.

2. You Talk Behind Their Backs

Here is some very simple advice - Talking negatively about your team to other people in your team NEVER ends well. They always find out and you lose the respect of almost everyone in that team. If you have a problem with someone's behaviour, feedback to them, not their colleagues!

3. You Don't Treat Others The Way You Want To Be Treated

How you treat others will directly link to how others treat you in return. This means you should be mindful when you decide how you want to be treated. Then give those behaviours to those around you, allow them to feel the way you want to.

For example, the manager I spoke to yesterday, liked to be the 'mother' figure within her team. Taking on all of the motherly duties and treating her team like her children. So guess what happened? Her team were treated like children, so they acted like children.

No surprises, but that is not what you want as a manager. What she has now done is identified that she would like her team to be respectful and honest. She now has to answer the question: What are the behaviours someone would have to show for you to treat them as respectful and honest?

4. You Act First, Then Think

Something happens in a situation that you perceive as a lack of respect and then fire back in an emotional manner. Then later will think, 'Why did I say that?'

This is an emotional reaction and is highly unlikely you will get the response or outcome you want. This is because the response from those around you is likely to be an emotional one too.

If you want to ensure that you get respect, thinking about how you feedback is critical. This takes planning, not much, but it will take a moment or two for you to gather your thoughts and remove the emotion.

If someone is disrespectful to you, think about how you will respond. It doesn't need to be a fight and it doesn't need to be emotional. What needs to happen is that behaviour is modified going forward.
What specific behaviour and situation are you discussing? What was the affect of this behaviour? What would you like to see in the future?

5. You Hold Back Your Concerns, Until You Explode

This is the opposite of acting first, thinking later! These are the times you will effectively 'bottle up' all your feedback and emotions, as the lack of respect builds and builds. Until, one day, all the emotion and feedback comes flooding out - probably for something and nothing!

If you let this happen, it is not the perpetrators fault, it's yours. Allowing poor behaviour or emotions to build and then exploding into an emotional feedback volcano, guarantees a failure to get respect.

The advice is the same as earlier - upon witnessing disrespectful behaviour, take a moment to remove the emotion and approach the situation factually. Then take the appropriate action as soon as you can.

6. Your Deeds Don't Match Your Actions

One of the quickest ways to lose respect of the people around you is to say you will do something or say that you stand for something and then don't. The best approach is to be mindful. To think about what you say and how you say it. The more people you lead, the more mindful you have to be.
Be clear and check understanding. If you do what you say you will do, respect will follow.

Putting it all together
We all want and need respect, especially in a management or leadership role. If you want to change the behaviour of the people around you, then you must change your behaviour first.

Remember, respect is earned, so transform your behaviour and you will transform the respect you receive.

The Challenge

To become the best leader you can be, you will need to be brave enough to put your current leadership up against a mirror.

However, most leaders don't bother. They think there is little else to learn... **They are wrong.**

The Solution

I had the privilege to speak at a conference about motivation and, as always, I stuck around to see the whole event. I was struck by this company's culture, they were progressive, enabling and it appeared as though they had a highly engaged team. They challenged their leadership culture openly - with the desire to improve as the main priority.

This demonstration of leadership behaviours highlighted an unconformable truth. Cultures and leaders like this are rare. Really rare.

How many senior leaders do you know that openly practise and develop their understanding of the science of human motivation?

They are literally an endangered species.

"Enlightened leadership is awareness where we experience values like truth, goodness, compassion and also intuition, creativity and focused attention"

Deepak Chopra

Even in our enlightened world, the most common approach you will experience from a leaders is, **"This is want I need from you."**

Most leaders ask for more, demand more, without giving to their employees. **Leaders want more, faster, cheaper and they want it now**.

Sometimes they might even throw in a financial incentive (Which has been proven to worsen performance when partaking in complex tasks - as proven by hundreds of social science experiments!)

So think about this for a moment - **Most leaders will ask their followers for improved performance and then provide them with an incentive that is a performance inhibitor!**

Now take a look at your own leadership - Is your approach a "this is what I need from you" one? Do you provide your followers with tools and strategies that support or inhibit them? How do you even know?

The world is changing and so are followers. Back in the time of the dinosaurs, a leader was seen as powerful and strong if they demanded more. Dinosaurs are extinct and so should be that type of leader.

Followers are demanding a new type of leader. A leader who is enlightened, a leader who understands social science, who understands intrinsic motivation and has the approach of **"This is what I will be for my followers."**

The absolute final truth about your leadership ability is in the hand of your followers. It is the ONLY factor that counts - **Your followers decide if you are a leader, nobody else.**

As a follower - What type of leader would you want to be lead by?

You will find that your answer gives you clues to the leader you need to become.

What is leadership, if it is not about creating the optimum environment for followers to be successful?

Think about YOUR leadership. Do you demand more from yourself in providing the conditions for your followers to flourish?

Be a true leader, be a progressive leader, **be an enlightened leader**. It is what the world needs.

The Challenge

Emerging leaders either think that it is nearly impossible to stand up for what they believe in or that it is one significant event that has to be instigated.

In short, emerging leaders don't know how to successfully stand up for what they believe in

The Solution

Rosa Parks, Nelson Mandela, Martin Luther-King - they are names of people who will go down in history for standing up for what they believed in and they help change the world in the process.

We are told these stories about how great people changed the course of the world by standing up to the status quo, sometimes facing insurmountable odds and winning.

We are told we can do this too. That we can make a difference, but can we? I mean can you go up against your line manger or the authority figures at work and not damage your career?

I think we can, but not the way the stories would have you believe.

Standing up for what you believe in is not a single event - it's not a single moment. Instead it is in your everyday behaviours and actions. Here is how:

1. Clearly understand what you believe in
2. Share this with everyone
3. Make sure everything you do is linked

So if you believe that, "you shouldn't tell lies"... then tell everyone your belief and then make sure you always tell the truth!

It's a simple example, but hopefully demonstrates the power of being able to stand up for what you believe in, because if this is how you live your life, then it is easy to challenge the status quo when needed, because everyone will expect it!

This of course has its challenges, but what it allows you to be is authentic, strong and value led. Which ultimately all great leaders are.

If you don't live your life by these rules, then you will end up living your life by someone else's.

Be the best leader you can be, by standing up for what you believe in.

The Challenge

Emerging leaders shy away from difficult conversations with their teams, peers and line managers. Therefore never maximising the potential performance of themselves or those around them

The Solution

The fact is difficult conversations are… difficult.

We will all have to have them within our lifetimes, whether we are in a leadership role or not, so the best strategy is to prepare well and approach with a positive perspective.

Here are four ways to improve the output of difficult conversations:

1.   Remove Emotion

This is the number one factor of why difficult conversations turn into massacres - being emotionally driven.

By definition, as challenging conversation will be emotive for at least one person - you will probably have adrenaline flooding your system too, if you are expecting a tough time. This is not helpful.

What is helpful is to stick to facts rather than emotions - this allows the conversation to remain in reality. Reality is vital if you want a positive outcome to the discussion!

The best way to do this is - preparation. Understand the facts, but also rehearse the conversation. Practise saying what you want to say. The more you practise, the better you will get! Therefore, even if you have adrenaline pumping through your veins, you will still be able to deliver the facts in a calm manner, because you have rehearsed it so much.

It is also very powerful to approach the rehearsals and the conversation itself with a focus on service.

The conversation is aimed at a positive outcome, so an attitude of service will alter your style, you will be less defensive (which will lower their defences too) and will enable you to talk factually without it appearing as an attack.

2. Understand you don't know everything

You only know what you know and nothing more.

When you understand this truth, it will allow you to focus on conclusions rather than delivery. What I mean by this is that it is far better to get a positive outcome from the conversation, rather than just saying what you have to say without regard for the outcome.

So many people go into difficult conversations, busting to say their side of the story, so much so that it ruins the rest of the conversation.

If you enter the conversation with your main priority as positive action resulting from it, then you will be more likely to listen. You will be more likely to understand and you will be more receptive to the right course of action.

3. Make sure your facts are real facts

It is the oldest advice in the book, but the reason why is because it is the most important! Your facts have to have been observed and checked by you.

The moment you rely on second hand information, the conversation will spiral out of control.

Again this is why preparation is so important. If you don't do your homework properly, you are asking for trouble.

4. Give time and space

I have seen people utilise all the advice above, but then all that great work is destroyed with this common mistake. A tight time limit on the conversation.

You can make great strides, but if you have to cut the meeting off because of something else you have booked in to do, then you may as well not have the discussion.

Very simply, plan and prepare for the discussion to go twice as long as you anticipate and don't book in anything that can't be cancelled straight after it.

If the conversation is difficult for you, then it is difficult for them. Show them respect by giving them the time and space they need. They probably haven't done all the preparation you have, so give them the opportunity to work it out.

By doing this you will achieve the following:

1. Shows that you are interested in them and a positive outcome, which will reduce their emotional levels (remember emotion is bad in these situations)
2. Allows autonomy - Give people the time to come up with the right response, through their own judgment rather than emotion and 99.9% of the time they will.

Putting it all together

We will all have to face difficult conversations in our lives… and the bottom line is they are going to be difficult no matter what.

You can improve the quality of the conversation and the desired outcome if you plan and prepare -

remove the emotion, rehearse and aim to serve. Remember, you don't know everything, so focus on the desired outcome rather than focusing on just having your say.

Ensure your facts have been observed by you.
Give time and space to work it through properly.

The Challenge

Most leaders, emerging and established, don't understand what a strategy is. Thus, they never have one, which of course will inhibit long term potential.

The Solution

The term "strategy" is used in most businesses just to make things sound more important, rather than being genuine strategic measures - instead of a 'project meeting' we will have a 'strategic project meeting'... sounds much more sophisticated and important, doesn't it?

Most leaders and companies tend to have a clear goal/vision, but instead of a strategy, they will just list off a bunch of actions to achieve the goal. The first thing to understand is -actions are NOT a strategy.

As Alistair Campbell states in his book "Winners", for any vision to work long-term, it is essential to have a strategy. In very simple terms a strategy is the "HOW" individual/business will approach achieving their vision. When the approach is clear, it enables everyone to stay on track when stuck in the detail. It creates consistency and adds weight and focus to the actions taken to achieve the goal.

So what is a strategy?

Vision - This is the main goal of the company/individual - This will be often value led... the "WHY" we do what we do.

Strategy - This is "HOW" we approach the goal - What will be the thread that binds all of the actions/tactics together, to ensure everything is focused on achieving the goal.

Tactics - "WHAT" actions will have to take place to achieve the strategy/goal.

For example, for the author of this book:

Vision: To create environments where those around me can reach their potential.

Strategy: Focus on 'being the best version of you' - specifically within leadership and living a higher quality of life, by developing effective learning environments/programs.

Tactics: Write leadership books, Develop on-line training programs, one-to-one online coaching, develop motivational speeches.

Although a simplified version, hopefully you can see that my strategy will ensure that all my actions are intrinsically linked together, which will in turn allow me to achieve my vision in a consistent and structured manner.

So, what is your leadership strategy?

Take some time today, to challenge yourself on this -
Do you have a strategy? Or is it just a list of actions?

A great strategy can rapidly improve your chances of
success.

The Challenge

Emerging leaders fail to appropriately deal with jealousy in the work place - either their own or their colleagues.

The Solution

Once upon a time, there was a man who got jealous of his work colleagues every time they were rewarded, recognised, given extra responsibility or promoted.

I am ashamed to say, that man was me as my leadership career was emerging. I still don't quite understand why, it just burned me up inside every time.

The problem is jealousy is an ugly animal. Even when you try to hide it from others, it negatively impacts those around you. Which in turn will reduce the chances of you being the recipient of the reward etc next time... which will then cause even more jealousy.

Is there a hint of jealousy inside you about someone at work? Does someone always get the credit? Who is that blue-eyed boy or girl that can't do any wrong? I mean, you work just as hard as they do, probably harder... why aren't you seen like they are?

Jealousy is ugly and it serves NOBODY... especially not you. Here is how to rid it from your life:

It's not jealousy, it is fear:

Fear has lots of different disguises and jealousy is one of its favorites. In this form it will either be one of two things:

1. Personal insecurity 2. Unfair comparison.

Either way it boils down to a fear that you are not good enough. Comparing yourself to others can be useful to measure progress, but when it is used to decide if you are worthy, it is venom.

Once you understand and take accountability that jealousy is really your fear, then you can identify what you are fearful of. Don't avoid it, fear feeds off that.

Instead identify it and start making small steps to shrink it. The absolute fundamental truth is, that fear will always play a part in your life. It is how you respond to it which will defines you.

Will you let fear cause you pain or will you take responsibility and ensure you take your fears head on?

You deserve some credit:

Do you know how amazing you are?

Take a moment to look back through your life, all the challenges, disappointments, successes and compliments. You have got through the tough times and you have created some good times.

That deserves some credit. That deserves some appreciation. Give yourself the recognition you deserve.

You are stronger than you realise.

When you give yourself permission to look back on your life and acknowledge how much you have been through and how special you truly are, then you will begin to worry less about others' perceived achievements because you know you have achieved amazing things too.

Give genuine best wishes to all

Leadership is not about being better than anyone else. It's about being the best version of you.

Focus on development, focus on growth, focus on learning from others. When you do this you realise that you can learn from everyone and everything.

While you are learning you are getting better, which in turn gets you one step closer to being the best version of you.

The best version of you isn't in competition with others - the best version of you wants everyone to do well. If someone gets a promotion over you, the best thing for you to do is to wish that person well and want to learn from them - not feel angry, jealous and sour inside.

You might think that this isn't possible, because some people just don't deserve success. I ask you, who is jealousy serving?

Does it make you feel good?
Does it stop the target of your jealousy?

Then why choose to feel it? It is your choice.

Jealousy is like drinking poison and hoping your enemy will die... It just doesn't work!

You know that being happy for others and focusing your energy on personal growth is the better way forward.

Putting it all together:

Jealousy is an ugly, hurtful feeling... which only affects you.

Look under the skin of Jealousy and you will find fear and vulnerability - identify this, accept this and face this. You can beat fear this way.

Also give yourself some well-earned credit - you have been through a lot and you are still here! That is amazing!

Finally, switch your focus from "they don't deserve" to "I must improve" mentality. The ONLY thing you have in your control is your emotions, thoughts and actions, use them to benefit you, not harm you!

The Challenge

Many emerging leaders use threats as a part of their management tool-kit.

The solution

I have just witnessed some of my friends go through a redundancy process - which has revealed an ugly and selfish reaction.

They were obviously and fiercely out for themselves, with very little care or thought to others around them. The bonds of team work disappeared during this process and it was heartbreaking to see. To witness the venom, to watch how they would stab each other in the back without a second thought was awful.

As the redundancy process finished, my friends assumed things would go back to normal - but they didn't.

The fear is still living. Nobody feels safe… and when nobody feels safe, they will not look out for each other and teamwork dies.

This is an extreme example, but it makes a clear point. The catalyst for the breakdown of trust is one key element - THREAT.

In my example, the threat was easy to identify, their jobs were put at risk. The instant reaction to this threat, was to go into self preservation mode and defend themselves.

How good do you think the team work was during this process? How about the customer service? How about training and development? How about sharing of best practice?

Zero - due to the threat.

Feeling under threat creates behaviours that are not conductive to high performance, especially over the long term. In fact, feeling threatened will destroy high performance.

Redundancy is a big and obvious threat, but there are others. More subtle threats that leaders make... Maybe threats that you have used.

What do your team think will happen to them, if you don't reach this period's sales target? Or ensure controllable spend is within budget? What do your team think will happen if they get audited? Or if a customer complaint comes in?

Are they growth opportunities or are they threats?

Because if you threaten your team - then YOU are eroding your teams performance level.

Threats reduce the circle of trust - and people who do not feel safe, who do not feel trusted… WILL NOT ACT IN THE INTERESTS OF THE TEAM AND WILL NOT PERFORM TO THEIR POTENTIAL.

The chances are you have used mild threats and didn't realise it could be fatal to your team. Any threat will have this effect, just the smaller the threat, the smaller and more gradual the reaction.

If this is something you have done in your leadership role, then here is what you have to do in order to restore the circle of trust with your team.

1. Apologise

I realise this will not be popular advice - particularly for those in leadership roles. The idea of a leader admitting they got something wrong, means they would have to show vulnerability. Which, if we are honest, most leaders don't do.

Even in today's enlightened world, where the benefits of authentic leadership have been scientifically proven… It is still incredibly rare to find a leader who is brave enough to show genuine vulnerability.

However, if you want your team to feel trusted, to feel safe and to work at their potential, with the success of the group at heart - then you will have to apologise if you have threatened them. It is the only way to open the gate of the circle of trust again.

Think of it from a follower's perspective - what is more motivating? A leader who lets past threats hang over their team OR a leader who correctly identifies poor behaviour, apologises for it and looks to find a better way forward.

I know which leader I would prefer to work for.

2. Re-frame

The reason leaders threaten is obvious. The leader wants to improve performance and create a sense of urgency in their teams. It is not that they are bad leaders who want to cause pain and suffering to all those who work for them. No - most of them just want to generate better results.

And in the short term, this can work. But it will NEVER last - it can't.

What is needed is a positive re-frame: transform from threatening tactics that extrinsically motivate to high performance environments that intrinsically motivate. A leader will need to identify and then implement the best possible environment for their team to perform at the highest level possible, over the short-term AND long-term.

There are many different strategies a leader can undertake. My personal advice on how to create a high performance environment - ask your team.

They are the only people who absolutely know what would motivate, inspire, make them feel safe and valued. They know what environment would make them achieve their potential and have the interests of the group in all of their behaviours.

3. Demonstrate you have their back

Actions speak louder than words - The leader who encourages creativity. The leader who will ensure their team is safe. The leader who works hard to ensure their team have the tools and environment to do their work to a high standard. The leader who will take accountability when times are tough and give credit when the good times roll in, is the leader who has a team that will shed blood, sweat and tears for them.

The leader sets the tone - you can either set a tone that breads fear and stress or you can ensure they feel protected and valued.

Putting it all together

We live in a high stress world, where nothing seems to be good enough. As a leader, if you allow your team to feel they are never good enough or threatened in any way - you are destroying the potential performance level of your team.

When your team doesn't feel safe, they will not be creative (too much chance to stick out and get punished), they will not be collaborative (Don't want anyone else stealing their ideas), they will not have each other's backs (pointing out others' failures stops the focus being on them), they will not perform (Do the minimum and stay out of trouble).

There is another way - build a circle of trust and value with your team. Create an environment where they can be at their very best.

The top 5 mistakes managers make with a new team & how to avoid them

The business world is dynamic, fluid and fast paced - and because of this, managers in today's world have to be able to adapt to new teams quickly and often.

The tangible benefits of connecting to a new team quickly can make a dramatic difference to a manager's success, progress and even career. Do it well and the opportunities are abundant. Fail to connect and the consequences could be dire.

The problem is that building yourself into a new team isn't as easy as it sounds. The traditional viewpoint would be this: The manager is the focal point of any team and all team members will comply and deliver on the way of working and behaviours expected.

This perspective falls short today. If a manager thinks they can rely on their job title alone in order to integrate into and build a high performing team - they are guaranteed to fail... dramatically.

In today's world, followers demand more than just a pay-packet to give themselves fully.

Followers demand (and rightly so) a leader with purpose, a leader who works to enable them, a leader who cultivates autonomy and a leader who strives to allow their followers to be the best they can possibly be.

I have worked as a follower and as a leader in many different teams and here are the 5 biggest and most common mistakes I have either made myself or seen in others.

If you want to engage a team quickly and effectively…

DON'T PANIC

When you inherit a new team the pressure is on… You have to deliver results from day one. Everyone has to improve. Your boss needs to see you have made an impact. Everything needs to be perfect.

Wrong! None of the above is reasonable.

If you believe everything has to be perfect, then your decision making will be erratic and confusing for your followers. You will be so busy second guessing what your boss wants, you will send your followers into a spin.

I know of a manager, that was so preoccupied with being perfect with her boss, that she made her team attend four meetings about the same thing, just so she could say her plans where aligned to what her boss thought… The problem was, this took four days away from work for her followers AND none of it ever came to fruition because her boss was just sharing ideas, rather than expecting her to action every word!

DON'T THINK THAT YOU ARE THE CENTRE OF THE UNIVERSE

The team you inherit are busy people, who have a job to do - don't expect them to treat you like a god, you're not!

If you expect your team to drop everything for you at the drop of a hat, you will lose them forever... They might turn up when you ask them to, but will they give you their blood sweat and tears? Never... They will give you their job description at best!

When first embedding yourself into a team, give one thought to your teams work load and patterns before you start demanding their time. Just taking a moment to think about others, will gain respect and engagement in spades.

DON'T THINK YOU KNOW BETTER

The most common mistake ever... the manager thinks they have a better way of working and better ideas than their team.

This is rarely true. The fact that anyone believes that they, as a single person, are smarter, better and more creative than a group of people (otherwise known as your team) is ridiculous and solely driven by ego.

I once had a manager who came in to manage a high performing sales team and who decided that to improve sales each site had to have a whiteboard with daily targets on. Not a bad idea in itself, but bring it into context to this manager's team and it suddenly became pathetic... This team didn't need to be told what to do to drive sales... they needed to be asked for their ideas and creativity.

Needless to say, those whiteboards never made an impact.

As a manager, you should be the best manager in the team... that's it. Your job is to understand your team, motivate your team and allow your team to work out the best way to deliver exceptional results.

Your job is not to have all the answers - I hate to break it to you, but you don't know it all - and your team know it!

DON'T FORGET YOUR TEAM ARE PEOPLE

When the pressure is on, it is easy to forget about the human element and instead see your team as resources rather than people.

As I have already explained, today's followers won't allow you to treat them this way and still give you exceptional results. Today's followers need connection from their leader - not barked orders.

When you start with a new team, the most important thing you can do, as a leader, is get to know them as people and let them see you as the individual you are - which when you feel under pressure could feel like a lot of time wasted… It is not!!

Your overall success will be based on your relationships. If you don't invest the time early, you may never build the level of success you desire. Relationships with your team are critical, give it the time it deserves - in fact give it double the time it deserves, then you will be paid back 10x what you put in.

DON'T PICK ON ALL THE NEGATIVES

This has close links to trying to be the know-it-all… Some managers, to try and gain credibility with a new team, labour over the numbers and pick out any that are below average to challenge each individual.

All this does is make your followers think you are a micro-manager… and if you didn't know micro-management is not a desirable way to lead.

Please don't think I am suggesting you shouldn't know your numbers, you MUST! The difference is in HOW you discuss them with your team. Rather than just challenging specific results, instead have a conversation about their role and performance - asking open questions. Do this skillfully and your follower will be explaining the challenges, solutions and actions within 3 questions. Just an extra few minutes of your time will buy respect, engagement and improved results... isn't that worth the effort?

PUTTING IT ALL TOGETHER

At some point you will have to inherit a new team. The quicker and more effective you are at building yourself into that team, the more successful you will be.
The critical factor in the success of any team is its people - this has to be your focus as a leader.

Make sure you do these 5 things to build a high performing team quickly:

1. Give yourself and your team time and space - you don't need to solve the world problems in a day, so don't try.

2. Put your team at the centre of the universe - they are the people who will deliver for you, make sure you respect them.

3. Ask your team how they can improve - many minds working together are better than one. You

don't have all the answers, but your team does!

4. Give as much time as possible to building relationships. This is the foundation of all elite performance, so neglect it at your peril.

5. Be inquisitive - ask about their roles and their results. Get your team to identify their own challenges and provide their own solutions.

3 strategies that will accelerate emerging leader's growth

So there are no rules to leadership per say, but we do have principles. Three of which, if you applied to your leadership style, can make a massive difference to your leadership, your followers, your results, your world.

1. Do the scary stuff!

It's about challenging the norm. It's about creativity, vision and pushing the boundaries. It's about asking your followers to give up the comfortable. It's about setting a course of action that you don't know will work or be successful.

It's about putting your neck above the line, for the chance to create something amazing.

Like I said, to truly lead, to truly make a difference, you have to commit to do some scary stuff! Especially in this day and age where most corporate worlds like their leaders to be compliant and follow consistent process. Do you want to make a difference? Do you want to lead in the truest sense of the word?

Then commit to the action that is going to make that difference. Anything that feels different, will frighten most people, the leaders that commit are the leaders that change the world!

Isn't fear a human instinct that stops us getting into danger? Yes – fear does stop us doing stupid stuff - It can also stop us doing great things!

The fear of failure is not danger, it's how we learn, don't be afraid to learn!

Bottom line – Don't push yourself and do the scary then you won't achieve anything of real significance.

2. Care about your people

Genuine, massive, in the centre of your heart type of caring... not as team members, not as recourse. Care for your people as the individuals they are!

Genuine care, creates loyalty, inspiration, drive and innovation within followers. Have you ever had a leader that had genuine care for you? How did you feel at work? Did you do a good job? Think, if you made your followers feel cared for, would they do a good job for you?

This doesn't mean you have to bake cakes for everyone and ring after work every night to see if they have got home safe... It's caring about your followers' welfare, contribution, hopes, fears, desires and aspirations. It's about doing the right thing for your people long-term, rather than delivering the short term result.

This can't be faked and you can't hope your followers know you care.

It has to be true. So pay attention, find the common ground and do the right thing for people. A group of followers who feel protected, who feel cared for, who feel valued will deliver better results, more consistently than a team who don't feel that way.

3. **Intensity builds immensity**

Create energy and define the higher purpose everyday... It's an obvious statement, but followers look to their leader for direction, action and belief. The great leaders take accountability for this. Most just assume that teams of people will be self motivated and will understand the vision, the reason why. This is a critical error. Don't assume a thing, take accountability instead.

Talk about your vision every day. Link every single result, task and objective. Drop the activities that don't link to the vision and celebrate the behaviours and actions that are desirable.

In summary.

Nothing significant will be achieved by leaders without pushing themselves and their followers out of the comfort zone and doing something scary.
To truly lead you have to truly care about your followers. Only then will you see the power within your people and don't leave your followers energy or purpose to chance, take accountability and link it to all they do.

The Challenge

Emerging leaders fail to consistently apply strategies that maintain personal high performance levels.

The Solution

How do some people, no matter what they do, perform at an amazingly high level? How do they seem to have so much energy, zest, passion and abundance in their lives?
What is it that they know, they do and they focus on to achieve and be so much?

We all have an opportunity to grow and become more, so no matter what point you are at in your life right now, this can amplify our performance and benefit us all. The best and biggest achievements in our lives come from within us. Focus on the right things and an exceptional life is in our grasp!

Why / Vision

A true understanding of why you do what you do, provides a sense of direction, clarity and purpose to how you live your life. The more clarity you have about who you are and the purpose of your life, the more chance you have of it becoming a reality! There are a number of ways to understand your why in more depth, however to get you thinking complete the following exercise:

Think of the 3 most important words that describe how you would like to approach life.

Now think of 3 words that you would most like other people to say about you after spending time with you.

These 6 words describe a version of you that is inspirational, of the person you want to be.

Then to keep this in your conscious mind, ask yourself, *"Am I living my highest self?"* *everyday.*

This keeps you focused on the person you want to be. It keeps you focused on your purpose in life. Once you are focused on something, you can make it happen. Focus on your highest self.

Presence

What I mean by this is to invest yourself in the moment. Not to focus on the past, not thinking about the future, not being distracted by non-important things. Invest yourself into NOW.

Your body, your mind, your focus all here NOW.

The number one difference between those leaders who are exceptional and those that aren't is presence.

Ask yourself daily:

"What level am I on a scale of 1 to 10 am I in my presence right now?"

Attention / Productivity

This isn't about getting through "to do lists". This is about putting attention on the areas that will progress your life dramatically and about putting attention on the important rather than the urgent.

We tend to live our lives today being busy, really busy. How much of our time we give to ourselves and our purpose takes a back seat and other people's agendas come first. That is just wrong!

Take back what you focus on. Focus on the important. The saying is true... 20% of the actions to do will achieve 80% of the results desired. What is the 20% in your life, in your purpose that will get 80% of the desired outcome?
DO THAT STUFF! I know it sounds simple... and it is. It's about not losing sight of who you are and what your purpose is and then putting your attention... your full attention on the things that matter!

Ask yourself everyday *"What is my mission today?"*

This will challenge your mind to think about the important aspects that need your attention... You just then need to commit your attention!

Communication with influence

Those people who change businesses, mobilise communities, accelerate people's growth, all influence in similar ways...

They challenge what is the conventional norm and they communicate with massive enthusiasm!

Being courageous in presenting your thoughts is vital to stimulate those around you. To create discussion, to enable imagination, to encourage creativity and to allow others to think differently. All of which are needed to generate real and lasting change!

Being enthusiastic in communication is contagious. Your enthusiasm spreads to others, it creates energy and it creates momentum.

Ask yourself everyday:

"Am I demonstrating bold enthusiasm?"

Physiology

It is hard to achieve anything when tired and fatigued. To be the leader of your dreams energy, passion and vigour are required! If you want more energy, if you want to feel more alive and be energised, then you have to eat well, drink lots of water, do exercise and sleep enough!
There isn't a secret recipe here. It's common sense. The highest performing people in the world know this and so do you.

There is lots of great advice about how to optimise your physiology, however for the purpose of this section we will keep it simple... Drinking water is key to ridding the toxins out of your body. Drink water and you will have more energy because you have less toxins.

Ask yourself daily:

"Am I hydrated?"

If this is the only thing you do, it will help your energy levels dramatically... However there are other aspects to feeling physically great, please invest in this. Feeling physically great is the platform for doing great things!

Adding value

The reason for living is giving. To feel completely fulfilled the act of being more, giving more, being a part of something more. This fills you up much more than any personal achievement.

I think we all know, deep inside, that giving back is massively important and will add more to our lives when we do. As a leader you can give back every day. You can feel bigger, bolder and better you every day!

"How can I serve greatly?"

Asking this will allow you to get outside of yourself, think differently and add more abundance

The Challenge

Emerging leaders misunderstand how to lead at a higher level.

The Solution

At some point in your leadership journey you will be given feedback that will ask you to demonstrate 'leading at a higher level.'

This type of ambiguous feedback isn't particularly useful, but it does pose a question that is worth considering, 'What is leading at a higher level?'

Leading at a higher level is helping people achieve their own potential and meaningful goals.

It might be a controversial thing to say in your business, but making money is not a worthwhile goal… However it is a by-product of leading well!

Those leaders, that lead with a meaningful purpose, those that lead to make the world a better place, make significantly more profit than those who just want to make a quick buck. Think about Steve Jobbs… he wanted to put a ding in the universe… or how about Bill Gates… he wanted to allow everyone affordable home computers. He didn't even make computers!

To continue this idea, there are two key focus areas:

Provide Hope

It sounds simple… focus on the positive and communicate a bright envisioned future. A higher level leader will make people feel valued and special. This doesn't mean lacking honesty. They are truthful about the current situation and if that situation is difficult, then they are honest. The difference is, that in that honesty they also give hope, give a vision, create togetherness and add value.

Your people are your business partners

When you lead at a higher level you understand that your people will know things that you don't. That they can support and help the leader.

Your people are everything. Treat them like they are a business partner not an employee. It is a subtle change in mindset, but it makes all the difference in creating the environment for your team to flourish.

Higher level leaders know that the combined intelligence of all of the team is much smarter than the single intelligence of the singular leader.

They know that their followers have deep knowledge and insight of the business they work in. They encourage, they all and they listen.

Leading at a higher level is about chasing worthwhile goals, being a beacon of hope and treating your team as partners rather than employees.

What do great Leaders actually do?

Leadership is one of the most complex and commonly debated topics in the business and management world today. Everyone has an opinion on what makes leadership and everyone will defend these opinions fiercely.

The reason why is, leadership is highly desirable. We all know true leadership can change businesses, industries and the world.

The problem is we can't all agree on what makes a great leader. The best leaders in the world, any leader for that matter, are all different and that is why we find it so hard to formalise what a leader should do.

I think the reason we find it so hard to formalise leadership is because it is not about the leader. Instead it is all about followers.

Followers choose to follow, they cannot be told or forced… **They choose.**

So, what do followers want?

Purpose

The best leaders I have ever worked with had a clear personal purpose or vision of who they were and what they stood for. They communicated this purpose as often as possible. If the leader had a purpose that linked closely with my values and beliefs, then I would instantly feel a deep connection and follow this leader with my heart and soul.

Enlist

A leader I am inspired by, is brilliant at recruiting people who shared the same values and beliefs as he did.
As a follower this was a fantastic experience. Being a part of a team who all had a common goal, not because they were told to, but because they wanted to created a huge amount of energy, passion and creativity. I can honestly say that a leader who surrounds themselves with the people who believe in their vision, pushed my performance and results higher than I could have imagined at the time.

Walk the talk

Simon Sinek articulated this beautifully when he described *'The celery test'* in his book **'Start with why'.**
Those leaders who walk the talk, who stand up for their values and will never compromise on those values to get a quick result. These are the type of leaders I love working for, I know they are authentic and I know they will have my back. As a follower, I feel trusted, so I give all of my trust freely to them.

Trust - the best leaders I have ever followed have always ensured that I had the skills and capability to do the task in hand and then allowed me to complete that task in my own way. In simple terms they trained, coached, supported and allowed autonomy. The power of supporting people when they need skills and capability and getting out of the way of those same people to allow creativity and ownership is significant.

As a follower I don't want to feel out of my depth and unsupported, yet I also don't want to feel as though I am being dictated to or controlled. The leaders that have found that balance, I have followed most passionately.

Encourage and Value

A really simple idea. As a follower, I like to know that I am adding value, doing a good job and my behaviours are positive. These factors, being rewarded with encouragement and praise, really boost my confidence and drive me to perform even better. However as a follower this needs to be conducted in an authentic and personal way to get the best out of me, so by that I mean it is not about incentives and bonuses... Don't get me wrong more money and prizes were nice, but they never made me work harder or inspired me like genuine encouragement would.

About the Author

I am a performance coach, motivational speaker and seminar leader with a passion for living an extraordinary life. This first book is an extension of my weekly blogs on www.daxmurphy.com

The purpose of my life is to help provide the environment for emerging leaders to inspire and motivate themselves to reach their potential, so they can become enlightened leaders.

I believe that the potential, in every individual, is massive.

What we are **CAPABLE** of doing is unbelievable. The opportunity is in how we apply ourselves, what we will accept... What we are **PREPARED** to do is the defining factor.

As individuals and as leaders we can create real, tangible and rapid change in ourselves and our people, if we have the right tools, application and environment to flourish.

Hopefully this book will help create that environment for you.

If you are interested in the concepts in this book, then please join me on my website. There are over 100 free videos and written posts designed to inspire and improve your leadership.

Thank you for taking the time to read this.

Become the best version of you!

Dax

22406156R00083

Printed in Poland
by Amazon Fulfillment
Poland Sp. z o.o., Wrocław